THE ALPHABET OF LOVE

Also by Bart Edelman

Crossing the Hackensack
Under Damaris' Dress

THE ALPHABET OF LOVE

Poems

Bart Edelman

Red Hen Press

1999

The Alphabet of Love
Copyright © 1999 by Bart Edelman

Red Hen Press is a division of Valentine Publishing Group.

Acknowledgments: "The Dogs of Amadeus," "Little Ghosts," and "The New Train" first appeared in *Chaparral.* "Black Pearls," "Bones of Silence," "The Book of Life," "The Dancer," "Footsteps," "The Great Dark," "Names," and "White Bird" first appeared in *Footsteps,* a limited edition from The Inevitable Press.

Special thanks to Susan Cisco, Mark E. Cull and Kate Gale.

Cover art: "Dragon Slayer"
       by Ilana Bloch, Los Angeles California

Author photograph: Jackie Houchin
Book design: Mark E. Cull

First Edition
ISBN 1-888996-09-9
Library of Congress Catalog Card Number: 98-86717

Red Hen Press
Valentine Publishing Group
P.O. Box 902582
Palmdale, California 93590-2582

for Arthur and Randy

TABLE OF CONTENTS

THE ALPHABET OF LOVE

The Alphabet of Love

A adores B,
But B is enamored with C,
C suffers terribly
From a protracted divorce with D
And won't get involved with anyone now;
However, C thinks E is fun
To help break the weekend monotony.
E seems mixed-up
And fell for F
Last month at a dance ranch,
Yet wonders why C hangs around;
Maybe G, a friend's sister,
Would be the best bet of all
Since the family is wealthy,
But E really has the hots for H,
Who runs around the track
Each week with I and J.
They both seem happily married to K and L
Although H knows the score:
I carries on at the office with M
And J spends each spare moment with N
When not making plans with O.
H thinks of lying low for a while,
Knowing full well P
Would take him back in a second.
(P wouldn't want him back again
For all the tea in China
But how could H know this?)
P is, in fact, being slandered by Q,
Who's upset by P's comportment
And lack of moral candor.
Q has decided to remain chaste—
"The only way to go these days"—
And thinks R, a former mate,

Might do well to heed the same words;
R entertained S and T
On consecutive evenings,
Feeling no shame whatsoever.
R advises Q that it's fine to play alone,
Everyone ought to have a choice;
Just the same though,
Perhaps, he might be willing
To speak to someone like U,
Who has a thriving practice
Over on the Westside of town;
After all, didn't they both date V
When they were in high school?
And speaking of V,
Wasn't that she on television last night
Throwing herself all over W,
Who walked out on X and their four children—
Despite the fact that they apparently
Had patched things up
Over W's affair with Y
(According to People magazine).
No, V is truly a blockhead —
And was never happier than the time
She and Z worked for the circus
(As jugglers and clowns)
When they lived in Manhattan.
If only Z hadn't taken that role
In the movie which filmed
On Bora Bora, starring A,
Everything would have been so simple—
But that was, alas,
Long before A came to adore B.

From the bottom of the sea
Twelve black pearls
Sang to me,
Each voice an octave
Higher than the next;
A dozen depths I dove—
Devoid of breath—
Closer to the precious stones
Upon the ocean floor.
Was I the first to see
This midnight cluster
Dance across the waves
And steal between the stars?
Carefully, I touched each gem
And felt the smooth, round skin
Roll slowly into my palm.
Dare I even ask
What divine creature
Opened its shell
To such perfect mystery?
And yet I knew
I did not possess
Either jewel, or key,
From which I could unlock
Ancient symmetry.
Under the shadow of glass
I floated a moment more
Before I swam to the surface,
Empty-handed—
My fingers glowing in the dark.

From the bottom of the sea
Twelve black pearls
Sang to me.

Once, each season,
When barking voices give way
To bones of silence,
I listen closely
For proof that I'm still alive.
I dig a six foot hole
In the cold, dark earth
And bury myself
Among the tightly packed pockets
Which form a perpetual line
Across my backyard.

After an hour, perhaps two,
The first sound I hear underground
Is nothing more than the truth,
Burrowing slowly towards me—
A timeless tunnel
Tracing the empty space
Between yesterday and today;
This constant struggle which pits
The forces of then
Against the wisdom of now.

Before long I sense
Cautious movement around me;
Small creatures take care
Not to disturb my resting place,
As if they know the secret peace
That lodges beneath the soil.
Soon, I am enveloped in sleep—
Deep enough to forget my name.
I awake the next morning
To the strain of a wailing howl,
And rise early—
Only to gnaw again.

He had cultivated
Love in a windowbox,
So high above the city
That he never saw the street.
Daily, his patient fingers
Nurtured the soil,
And watched seed
Slowly turn to stalk,
And stem become flower.
Here was goodness
He could hold
In the palm of his hand,
Bright sunlight which danced
Down a deserted hallway,
And crept across
The drab little room,
Where, page by page,
He pressed each precious petal
Into the book of life.

The crow came soon
To rest among feathers—
Cool to the claw,
Warm on the wing.

The crow did not know
How long it had been,
Since this downy bed
Tucked another bird
In the soft grasp of spring.

For all the crow cared,
It may well have taken
Nine beaks to build the nest,
But it was of no consequence.

When a lonely crow
Measures the black stars
Against a glass sky,
Nothing can safely pass
Between night and sleep.

The Dancer

Watch her begin to spin,
Turning circles in the air,
Floating like a feather
On the back of the wind;
Come, take a moment
To sit and observe:
The tilt of her head,
The swirl of her lips,
The sweep of her hands,
The curl of her hips;
See how rivers flow
Beneath her knees,
And lush gardens grow
Up through her toes;
Feel the beat of the street
As both feet kiss the floor,
Her city, never at rest;
And always there is undulation—
This perpetual motion—
The marriage of beauty to form,
Graceful strength newly born.

Day of The Locus

Amid the discarded shards of hope,
The twinkling glass
Shattered the roadway
That cradled Route 111 and Route 80
In the palm of a giant, unforgiving hand
Which finally closed
Midway between Calexico and El Centro;
There wasn't even a moment
For them to say goodbye.

Eileen's watch stopped at 2:55
On December 22, 1940,
As she lay twisted in a ditch,
While Nat toiled with his last breath,
Gasping on the asphalt.

For both of them
Time ceased to exist—
Gone were the books, the hunting trips,
And the children who would never be;
The wedding dishes, still packed,
Lay at home in boxes,
As if they somehow knew
Destiny had no business eating breakfast.

They had waited a lifetime for each other
And now West had failed
To yield the right of way,
Ignoring the only glaring sign
On that Sunday afternoon,
Trading his belief in the party dress
For the politics of the open road,
Dangling behind the lethal wheel.

And when it came to pass,
It certainly wasn't the crash
Of the 30s that killed them,
But a Pontiac sedan
Driven by a fruit tramp
Whose hand West would have gladly shaken
On any given night.

For what ultimate purpose
Was the locus of fate formed,
If not to crack the clock
That bled drop by drop,
Out along the lonely boulevard.

Had the gods bothered to look down
That cool winter day,
They might have seen
A million teeming dreams
Rising up to meet them.

(for Nathanael West)

Denial

Perhaps, it was foolish—
All this futile floundering
Across a frozen ocean—
One thousand three hundred and thirteen
Strokes of denial,
Each fear compounded
By the unreachable shore,
The absentminded tide
And the lure of exhaustion. . .
So far gone then—
What was I to see?

I felt myself failing
But railed against the dreadful
Unknown below me.
How many fellow souls
Had perished from reckless faith
Just when their trial began?
I would not belie
The intrinsic nature of man,
This pact handed down—
Father to son—
An unbroken line
Unmarked by time.
I was still treading hope
Until my limbs floated no more
And salt bathed my eyes.

Ultimately, a carpenter fish,
The most beautiful and sacred
In all the sea,
Caught me in its delicate jaws
And pulled me under.
But if I went for food,
So much the better;
No life remains lost
Where purpose bows to grace—
Surrender its own reward.

THE DOGS OF AMADEUS

The dogs of Amadeus
Bark night and day,
Now that the master's away.
You can hear them yelp
Clear across the valley
And over the next hill;
The scent from his skin remains,
But this is not enough
To make the creatures sane.
Only when we play his music,
Do they lay their heads
Upon the cold ground
And cry themselves to sleep.
Why he need keep
So many hounds around
Confounds each one of us.
Perhaps, it is better
Not to know such things.
When spring finally arrives
And he returns again,
All shall be well—
The dogs will wag their tails
And grow silent at his feet,
While we complete
What must be done,
If he is to compose the work
The world will one day hear.

Someone's been writing verse
Across the stark white walls
Outside the City Hall of Kiev;
Such words tell stories,
Hellbent on hope:
This is what is—
That was what was.
People, once shy and silent,
Slip pens in their pockets
And take the metro uptown
To add a stanza or two,
Before the querulous old guard
Comes snooping around the corner.
"Everyone's a poet these days,"
Sneers the deputy minister;
But even he scrawls his message
On the clean flat surface,
When he's alone at night—
After the sun sets—
And east meets west.

We wonder what it would be like
To reach out and nab one
As they fly through the air—
Grab it in our open hand
And turn it over,
Again and again and again,
Examining every part of its mystery
For any common clue to explain:
How it is set in motion,
What makes it soar,
Who designed its wings.
We struggle with complex answers
Which defy simple reason
And keep us safely on solid ground—
Dutifully bound.
But one spring day,
Sooner than we might imagine,
A man in a silk shirt
Will flap his spindly arms
In just the right way,
And, suddenly, he'll be gone—
Floating across a crimson sky at sunset,
Where children with wide eyes
Will gaze in momentary surprise,
Before they flutter home for supper
To tell an incredible tale.

FOOTSTEPS

If I listen closely enough
I can hear your father's footsteps
Gaining on you each day;
Sometimes, it's how you say your name
Or the way you tilt your head—
Side to side—
The subtle act of denial
That turns your smile upside down.

And when life runs too smoothly
You retreat to the kitchen's corner
As if you're waiting
For the next shoe to drop,
The open hand to fall
And slap you across the room.

Once, I admit,
I had the thought,
Perhaps, things would work
Better between us
If I just played the part
And kept the lie alive,
Twisting my tongue
Into a series of knots,
Swallowing these dirty little secrets—
One by one.

And he's coming next week
On the train from Florida,
Bringing with him
His eighth wife,
His mountain of debt,
His outstanding warrants,
And, of course, his bottle,
From which he'll pour you
A tall glass of shame;
And you will do nothing
To send him away,
For fear you'll lose
The tight-fisted glove
That grips his terrible love.

THE GREAT DARK

Agleam, aglitter, aglow—
Even the faintest star
Always knows how far
To cast its light
Around the unsuspecting moon.
What little hope remains:
We tuck inside a pocket,
Seal within an envelope,
Lock behind a door.
And, still, there's no guarantee
That what we see
Illuminates the great dark.
Could the firefly speak,
She would reveal
The story of her life,
Where day becomes night
With just the sudden flick
Of an internal switch.
If only it were that simple
For the rest of us,
Caught somewhere in midair,
Flying through the gloom—
Our fluorescent search begun,
Love's labor never done.

THE HOWL

What was that howl
We heard late last night—
A wail which woke us
And told some dreadful tale
We thought we left behind.

The haunting cry came
As quickly as it went,
Yet we remained still—
This nagging ring lingering
Long into the silence
We beat back with a stick.

How did it happen
That here, of all places,
The creature would know
Where to find us,
After we took a vow
To set things straight
And start life over—
Even against these odds.

Had we only been able
To listen more closely
And pinpoint the sound,
We could have captured
The lengthening shadow
Stretched between us;
But it was too late,
And the beast escaped—
Free to prowl again.

Imminent Danger

They've shot you
Full of holes again,
And you bleed
A little bit less this time;
Still, there's the sense
That imminent danger remains
A stranger in love
With the sound of your name.
So you plug on night and day,
Filling the gulf with words
The grandmaster would speak
If he were alive
To survive his own disaster;
But no matter,
For damage is damage,
Despite how it must be contained—
The art of flood control,
An improper science at best.

Tomorrow morning,
It's not Uncle Walt
You spy in the supermarket
Among the lemons, mangoes and melons—
Only Noah who's stocking up
Before the next deluge;
You ask him if it's possible
To book a reservation
This far in advance,
Yet he glances
At the empty bin of onions,
Drops his shoulders
And slinks away.

INVITATION

What I dread most is want—
That long drink of desire,
Undressed beside beauty's fire
And time's indisputable lie.
I close my eyes to love
And summon the breathless voice—
One distant cousin to another.

My invitation intrigues her;
She arrives under moonlight,
Faintly amused by the alarm
I've wrung from my heart.
She speaks softly of sailors
Lost somewhere at sea. . .
And if this is their fate,
Why must it not be mine?

Timidly, I turn from truth,
Rested and ready
To inaugurate the chasm of fear,
Growing wider at my feet.
I straddle life's jagged edge,
Awaiting ultimate denial,
While she paints her tapered nails
And cuts her red teeth
On my delicious shadow.

LAKE SUCCESS

Tightly packed in our cars,
The procession sped ahead,
Headlights out along the open road,
Engines straining ever faster
Over the tar-stained surface
That steered us through the pine forest
And around the banks of Lake Success.
Winding above the water's edge
We glanced below to discover
The glowing torches,
Flames which leapt up
To lick the darkened sky.
The pulsating sound—
Distant music uncoiled—
Told us that we had arrived
At revelation's front door,
The shoreline of good fortune.
Well-groomed attendants ushered us
Down to the smooth white sand
Where we paid our debt
To those who first set the path,
Turning one stone after another.
That indelible night we resolved:
Never to return home,
Never to stop at go,
And never to leave less
Than our footprints behind.

THE LATE NATALIE WOOD
(Visits the Church of the Good Shepherd)

I saw the late Natalie Wood
At Christmas Eve Mass last night
In the Church of the Good Shepherd,
Smack dab on Bedford Drive,
In the heart of Beverly Hills;
How curious to see her alive again!
There were flowers in her hand,
And she was wearing
A splendid black Chanel jacket,
And a lavender jacquard skirt.
At her side sat a man
No more than twenty years old,
Transfixed beyond measure,
Staring unabashedly at her,
Running his eyes through her hair—
From the opening rite
To the closing prayer.
Even normally cool Father O'Ryan
Seemed a bit taken aback
With the vision in the front pew,
But he couldn't place
Where he'd seen that face before. . .
Still, his intrigue remained
Until the final carol was sung
And the chant of peace exchanged.

When Natalie Wood rose to leave,
We stood there silently
And watched her stroll up the aisle,
Smiling at each one of us,
As if we had just been blessed
By the mere sight of her,
Passing through our lives
On this most holy night,
Where she suddenly appeared
To worship the birth of Christ.

(for Jackie)

Little Ghosts

This overwhelming sense of dread,
Damp tendrils wrapped tightly
Around children's heads;
Two doors slam shut
And she bolts up in bed.

It is midnight in Prague—
Bleary eyed, she leaves her room.
The front desk manager
Takes one glance at her
And knows where she's been.
He offers her tea
And leaves an extra glass out;
"It is for the little ghosts," he says,
"The children who slept here
Days before they were sent to Terezin
And later to find their fate at Auschwitz."

"You see," he explains,
"This was once a way station.
The young ones were kept at this place
Prior to their deportation.
They were, indeed, orphans,
The poor unfortunates who died twice—
First, when their parents were led away
Or shot in the street,
And, again, when the Gestapo
Trapped them behind these walls."
He states this rather methodically,
Without surprise to find her
Wandering sleepless at this hour.
"It is the malady of many
Who unknowingly board here.
The little ghosts reveal themselves
Only to the ears and eyes of strangers."

The next morning
She approaches the desk
To check out early.
The manager has her bill calculated
Before a word is spoken.
She detects his wry smile
And hears a small voice call
As she steps into the past—
A familiar train at her back,
Belching smoke down the tracks.

THE LOCKET

Oh, to be encased
Inside a heart-shaped locket,
Gently resting below the neck
Of the woman I love,
So that she is free to see me
Whenever it pleases her.
There I would wait patiently
By light of day,
Or dark of night,
Just for a single kiss
And the warm breath
That escapes her lips.
Within a closed hand
She would clasp me tightly
And then slowly open the catch,
Revealing the only man
She can trust enough
To share her secret life—
Tender dreams of hope
She takes to bed each night.
With a delicate finger
And a wistful sigh,
I watch her carefully trace
The contour of my tiny face,
Before she shuts the case
And tucks me safely away—
For another day.

THE LOFT

Atop the stairs
The little loft sits,
Empty in the sunlight
Summer left behind.
Old shadows crawl
Across bare walls
And disappear from sight.
The dusty wooden floor
Cracks no more under shoes
Whose soles once taught
Each groove to speak.
The tightly closed window
Refuses to open,
Its crank broken—
Another season of use;
And the stale air
Smells vaguely familiar,
Redolent of work
Yet to be done.

MARK TWAIN'S CIGAR

Mark Twain's cigar
Glows in winter's gloom;
By a dim light,
Ringing the dark side of the moon,
He carefully writes,
"How poor am I
Who was once so rich!"
And closes the notebook
He will later call his autobiography.
Before he climbs into bed
He pours a jigger of brandy—
Prescribed by the doctor for his heart—
And drops slowly off to sleep.

In the recurring shadow,
Revealing a remarkable dream,
Five coffins await him
When he descends the stairs
And enters the kitchen for breakfast.
One by one, he reads the placards
Which sit beside the caskets,
But they make absolutely no sense;
Bending over the open boxes,
He finds each is empty,
Except for some unrecognizable photographs
That mean nothing to him—
Strange faces in silent rivers.

Returning home, later that day,
He is alarmed to discover
The coffins are now cradles
And the servants gently rock them,
Singing hymns as if they were in church.
Angrily, he demands the small beds be removed—
Yet then thinks better of it,
Realizing the wood can be put to good use;
He suggests it be immediately cut
And stacked in the carriage house.
The servants stare at him in horror,
But he can not understand their amazement
At such a simple and reasonable request.

Mark Twain awakes the next morning,
Dressed in yesterday's clothes,
Closely watching the angels
Carved in the magnificent headboard
He brought back from Europe.
Scattered ashes of regret
Lie across the oversized bed,
His mouth parched and thirsty
From the faint taste of tobacco leaves.
A half-smoked cigar
Rests in his right hand,
And he seems quite surprised
To find himself alive.

Modern Man

Standing on the ledge,
A floor above Wall Street,
Modern Man proposes
Love on demand—
The stock exchange of bartered souls
Immune to price control;
Here, the platinum hearts
Stagger to outbid each other
Before the closing bell
Rings another session
To a merciful end.

From the shiny bow
Aboard his sleek new yacht,
Modern Man imposes
Respect upon command;
His stern, stiff salute
Welcomes a somber crew
Who walk zombie-like
To their appointed stations,
Holding each breath with both hands,
The silent ship sailing slowly
Around the Cape of Mediocrity.

In a dimly lit studio
Across from Freedom Hall,
Modern Man composes
His sonata of sand—
The grand plan—
Where he is saved in the wick of time
By the holy redeemer. . .
Free now to justify his life,
He takes a holiday,
But soon returns
To orchestrate his own demise.

NAMES

Say your name twice,
Repeating each syllable
Softly and slowly, at first,
As if the world would be
A lonely space without it;
Ask yourself why
You were given this name
And trace it
On the back of a leaf,
Or down the edge of a stem,
Touching every letter
With the tip of your tongue.
Now, wonder aloud
What you would lose
And who you would be
If this familiar name
No longer belonged to you
And was bartered away
On the price of a song.
For when life seems too busy
With people and places and things
That make you question
Why you are here,
Then write your name
In the warm rain
The night left behind,
And always know
It will be waiting
To follow you home.

THE NEW TRAIN

The new train travels
Swiftly over tarnished tracks,
Budapest no longer some distant dream
Or dot on a map.
Time slides back to reveal
The rolling hills of spring,
Caught midway between seasons—
Too sleepy for change.

Just outside of Brno,
Daisies grow wild in the sun
And cover mile after mile—
A carpet of golden hope—
As far as the eye can see.

At Breclav, a young transit policeman
Asks for proof of citizenship,
Decidedly eager to show
His proficient use of English;
He checks our passports
And laughs at the photographs.

Time wanes and turns to haze.
In the glass corridor
Where forgotten dreams remain,
We reason why we journey here,
And cross each silent bridge—
A trestle closer to tomorrow.

Approaching curious Bratislava,
The new voice of Slovakia
Whispers a clever secret
Out among the green fields
And tiny vineyards which stretch
Along the gentle slopes,
Winding through the countryside.

With Budapest on the horizon
And the Danube's blue water
Curled like a child beside us,
We ride into the heart of Hungary,
Tracing our way home—
One rail at a time.

THE OLD LIE

That old lie,
Folded over your shoulder,
Month after month,
You presumed would keep out the cold;
Now that you've come clean,
I'm expected to understand
It had nothing
Whatsoever to do with me,
As if I were never here—
An apparition trapped
In a sideshow mirror
Along the midway.

You who dropped
This atomic ring of truth
Are surprised the fallout
Swirls around us still;
You suggest I visit a specialist—
Someone to level my head—
Or ask the pharmacist
For a miracle balm
To rub into my skin,
Which will shrink the wound
And make my flesh pink again.

I could learn to forgive
If I believed you noticed
The tiny zone in me
That is dead,
And went to its grave long ago.
How silly of me
Not to see the shroud
I've prepared for myself,
This daily ritual
By which I deny
The clothing I wear—
The closet of black shoes,
Always one size too small.

Piano Lesson

They told me
You'd come once more—
Just after I'd left—
To climb the stairs
And walk the floors;
He said you lingered a while,
Your arms thin,
Your step unsteady;
Perhaps, you paused to smell
The sweet scent of pine
With another year
Ground into its grooves.

She thought you looked lost,
But how could that be?
You who first found the place
And kept it warm for me,
You who dressed each room
In clothes braced for the cold.

I wish you'd called,
So as not to alarm them;
I think it was a bit of a shock
To see you again,
Yet I understand why you went—
Really, I do;
It's just that they've been quite good
About the maintenance
And lending a hand.
One day they confessed
They weren't strangers to trouble.

Last week, they asked
If I planned to return;
I made it clear
The key was for keeps—
Like you said that night:
Who needs an autopsy?
All the same,
I'm sorry for the scenes;
I'd like to think
That wasn't you and me
Who screamed such things.

He felt I should know
You inquired about the piano—
Was it being put to use
And not just taking up space
In the corner of the living room?
I mentioned to them
I'd send for it later
When I had a larger place;
I still hope to practice
My scales one day.

It's almost midnight
And I need to be at work
Early this entire month,
You know, with tax season and all;
I'll get the other mail off by tomorrow.
It seems odd addressing you
Through nothing but notes—
A fate I've learned
To measure too late.

THE POLICEMAN'S WIFE

The policeman's wife
Shadows me across the room,
Searching for clues
In every line I read.
She watches me—
Week after week—
Counting down each day
Until the semester snaps shut,
A hungry set of jaws.

The policeman's wife
Thinks I ought to know
What she was before,
And what she is today.
The power of the word
Has turned her loose
To walk the naked streets,
Her only crime her skin—
A rash of wasted time.

The policeman's wife
Quivers ever so slightly
When she talks to me.
She sits in my office,
Her hand brushing my knee,
And I anticipate our future:
How many laws would we break?
How many states would we flee?
How soon would he find me?

The Alphabet of Love

The policeman's wife
Plans a secret rendezvous
Out along Highway 4321,
One week after the term ends.
"Are you game?" she asks by phone.
The offer sounds tantalizing,
But I weigh eternity behind bars
And cop a pitiful plea,
Before I blot her out of my life.

The Reading

You wonder what they know,
Curled up, row by row,
Fine tuning you in and out—
Each fork pitched back
Under the light of darkness.
You speak for fifty minutes
And measure your height
By the polite applause
Which follows the reading.
The customary break ensues
Where you wolf down
A cookie or two
And a cup of coffee
Before the questions begin.
A man in a red beret
Insists that your style reflects
A certain experimental school—
One that you're quite unfamiliar with;
You say you're unaware of this connection,
But he refuses to buy it,
Claiming he's midway through an article
Based on your books—
And he can prove it,
If given just five minutes.
Nevertheless, the punctual moderator
Graciously moves the program forward.
A provocatively dressed woman
Rises quickly from her seat
To ask if sex is the natural link
Between the body of your work;
You stare at the short length of her skirt
And agree that it might be the case.

An elderly gentleman requests you read
A poem you wrote about a city
He was born in eighty years ago;
You gladly oblige,
Taking particular care to smile
When you mention the city's name.
For almost an hour
You field questions which range
From form to figuration to fidelity.
By evening's end
Only half the audience remains,
Yet they purchase every available book,
Assuring you'll sleep tight tonight
In room 606 of the Holiday Inn.

REFUGE

The only refuge she knows
Closes for winter vacation
In less than a week;
As my mother would say
She is quite beside herself,
Fearing another upcoming depression
She can pinpoint down to the minute.
Suddenly, we are no longer talking
About a final exam or grade,
But her life,
Hanging in the balance,
Suspended on a wire,
High above the arena,
While the ringmaster requests
The safety net be removed.

She tells me the vacant time—
A month of disembodied days—
Will surely kill her.
I start frantically pulling books
From atop my office shelves,
Anything to help her
Occupy the long hours,
Yet she is convinced this will not do;
Only *The Bell Jar* interests her.
I immediately worry
She will crawl so far into Plath
That she may never walk
Out of the kitchen again.

She leaves with a few novels
Tucked in her knapsack
And a collection of Czech drama.
I promise to call
During the extended break.
She is surprised to find
Professors are routinely furnished
A list of student phone numbers—
For emergency purposes, of course.

THE ROAD TO JERUSALEM

Pale and silent she lay,
Eyes straining to find
The sacred spot on the wall
Where God and man
Converged to tell all,
Etched in the promise
Eternal life traced
On the face of pain.

How many hopeless years
Had she stumbled blindly
Across deserted plains—
So vast and empty
That only the morning hymn
And the evening prayer
Taught her to survive.

The small wooden door
To her cloistered room
Crept open with each gasp
She drew between her lips,
Pressing them closer together,
As if she were kissing
This world goodbye.

And then the vision came,
Without chariot or thunder—
Trumpet or drum—
Among a grove of pines
The benevolent son stood,
Both arms outstretched,
Offering the most magnificent hands
She had ever seen.

Above an unmarked plot,
Where one good woman
Found her long awaited rest
In earth's green shadow,
Children dance and sing
Heavenly songs to saints,
Who walk beside Jesus
On the road to Jerusalem.

SALMON

I'm not the same man
She married, she tells me,
And I think, surely,
I must have descended
From a long line of wayward salmon,
Spending half my life
Hanging in the air—
Mid flight—
Afraid of landing fin first.
How strange to know now
That what I first imagined as love
Was just a cruel fish
Spawning its way upstream,
Directionless and unschooled,
In the scheme of it all.
But she. . .
Is it possible?
Could she have seen
The curiously colored net
Which glowed in the despicable hand
The angler set forth,
After the whirling reel
Committed its unspeakable crime?
And if she grasped
This ultimate sense of doom,
Why had she not dropped
Through the surface
To the depths below?

SHADOW

And when she left
My shadow wept
And walked the streets for weeks;
It was bad enough
With the girl gone,
But a lost shadow
Is a far more serious matter.
What would people say
About a man who had no control
Over his own reflection?
I searched wherever
We went together:
Down each winding road,
Out the usual back alleys,
And through the city parks;
From sunrise to sunset
My feet bled blood red,
But I couldn't give up.
I placed ads in the local paper,
Listing names and clues
Which only he would know—
I offered to purchase
The cashmere sweater he'd ogled
For a dozen Christmases,
Yet I never heard a word,
Not even the normal silence he spoke;
Had he truly vanished?

● ●

Months passed like molasses. . .
And then as luck would have it
I saw them together
Late one evening—
The two ingrates,
Sipping strawberry daiquiris
By the water's edge—
Out in public, no less!
I couldn't believe my eyes,
But there they sat,
Tight as a tourniquet.
I confronted them directly
And they denied nothing;
There wasn't an ounce of shame
In either of them.
They bought me a drink
And held my hand
When I suddenly broke down,
Without so much as a warning.
We spent hours together—
I was oddly entranced;
Really, I had to admit,
They made a charming couple.
I explained my predicament,
The source of my sorrow—
How I'd taken unfair advantage of them both
And said I'd do anything to prove myself;
But when I finally left,
I could taste their pity.

● ● ●

The contract arrived mysteriously
In the next morning's mail;
It was a rather thorough document,
Drawn up by a team of lawyers.
I was to support them both
For the rest of my life,
And, in return,
I was to receive
The company of my shadow
During the daylight hours,
While my girl was entitled
To his services from dusk to dawn;
What could I possibly do?
I signed the papers immediately,
Put in for the graveyard shift at work,
And lived happily ever after.

SISTERS

The dull sister
Wore a twisted smile,
Revealing a row of false teeth
And a decayed bridge,
From which she contemplated suicide
Almost every afternoon,
When she was not chasing
The mailman down the road—
Like a bloodhound—
Her keen sense of smell
Sniffing the perfumed letters
Sweethearts sent across the state.

The wicked sister
Denied she had a sibling
And worked at Woolworth
Behind the shiny silver counter,
Serving grilled cheese sandwiches
Each sweltering day,
While she spent evenings
In the motel rooms of hungry men
Who paid handsomely to see
How she split her sex
Before their startled eyes.

The morning they were found
Inside the small frame house
On the outskirts of town,
They were locked in a lover's embrace,
Joined by the separation
Which kept them apart—
Troubled no longer
By the complication of birth:
A father's wrath
And a mother's silence;
So that in the end
All they knew was each other.

SKYLIGHT

Here is the skylight—
Ever slightly ajar;
A tiny ray of faith
Trickling down to the ground.
I pick up a piece of hope
And feel how easily
It settles in my hand,
So much more alive
Than when I was a child
And grace seemed out of reach,
Even in the clean white church,
Where we were taught to pray
For all the dead souls
Who longed to be saved.

Now that I am older,
Neither Sister Mary
Nor Brother Mark
Dictates any offering I make
To the heavenly power
Which paints each leaf
The color of life.
Only a cracked window,
Suffused with light,
Guides me over the path.

STORIES

We tell them often:
To pass the time,
Share some new joy,
Hush an old grief,
Teach a lesson.
It is, perhaps,
The only moment
When we remain children,
Listening intently
For a beginning,
A middle
And an end;
Sustaining belief,
At least in that instant,
When all seems possible
And no world is without
A complimentary admission.
Each day of our lives
We are privy to stories—
Unblemished by lies
And the invisible lines
Which separate fact from fiction.
By nightfall's edge
We crawl safely back home,
Where we breathlessly watch
All the news that's fit to print
And then retreat to sleep,
Waking early the next morning,
Eager to turn the page again.

SWINE

I spoke of reality
And the joke was on me. . .
"Whatever is begotten, born and dies"
Sounds far more wise
Than the Sunday school
Lies they tell to keep you holy
The other six days of the week.
Think of it this way:
You're a pig in a pen
And you know your nights are numbered,
But you still oink
And boink with the best of them
Because your pink skin
And your blunt nose
Cannot camouflage the fact
That you're nothing more
Than a domesticated boar
To those around you,
No matter what you do.
So, it's probably best
To slip in there with the swill
And get what you can
Before it's gone;
After all, the essence of life—
The very self-actualization
Which determines our existence—
May be nothing more
Than the daily box scores
And a pile of slop
Strewn among the swine.

Ten Years From Now

One imagines her—
Ten years from now—
Entertaining an old man in Lyon.
She stands on a balcony
Outside her apartment,
Summoning the wild birds
That flock from the town square
To nest in her hair.
And he, amused,
For the first time
In an inglorious age,
Laughs so unpredictably loud
That the neighbors wonder
What this mistake must be.

Later, when the sun's shadow
Releases the inviolate moon,
She longingly bathes him
In a lotion of honeyed lavender
And teaches him the proper way
To make love to her.
The next day at dawn
They find him
Dressed in his tender reward,
Asleep on the feathered bed,
Cradled in her arms.

The Terminal of Grief

In the terminal of grief,
Your only relief
From the runaway train
Steaming down sorrow's track
Is a paper heart,
Attached to the shirt
Which covers your back.
By now, you think
Someone would have spied
The telltale sign,
And marked it with a bull's eye—
But love is harder to find
Than the hijacked caboose,
Abandoned out by line 99.
All day long,
You wait and pray
Under the artificial light
That paints each passenger
A pale shade of gray—
No less ghastly
Than the ghostly apparitions
Who stop to haunt
The rolling stations of the cross.

THE THIN WIRE

Through a tiny speaker
The voice stammers,
Turning each table,
Rearranging our lives.
For a sudden moment,
Words are nothing more
Than syllables lost in space,
Eager to find earth;
Yet once the terrible cargo
Lands upon that empty field—
We are strangers in the window,
Children at the door.
Slow recognition leads us
Into winter's stiff wind,
Blowing the hats off our heads.
Everywhere we look
There is little to see,
But the naked truth of trees
Mourning the loss of leaves,
Too brown to hang on boughs,
Just waiting to break.
Oh, if it could only be
As it always was—
To know we still belong:
In the old house,
On the same road,
By the green sea.
Now it vaguely seems
An improbable dream of chance,
This distant voice trailing
Over the thin wire.

THE VISIT

Last Friday night
He stopped by and told us
There was nothing more to write:
Thought he'd just about covered it all,
Retired his old black pens
And reams of white lined paper,
Bought a small place up around Saugus,
And figured to find God
Out among the sagebrush,
Somewhere off Old Highway 12.
He was ready to leave
The very next afternoon
And felt we should "know the score"
As he put it;
Didn't want us waking up—
One morning without proper warning—
To strangers living on his land.

We asked if he'd stay
For a cup of coffee,
But he claimed it was late.
When we offered to give him a hand,
He said what little he had
Already was packed the day before;
He just thought it was certainly
The neighborly thing to do—
This unexpected visit to our house—
And wished it had come sooner;
If he'd disturbed us, he apologized.
And then he was gone,
Disappearing into the night,
The lights of his pick-up truck
Glowing dimmer in the distance
As it lurched down the dirt road.

WATCH

Talk to them this Sunday,
When they line the park benches
And lift their grey heads
To see who's come out to play.
Tell them what life is like
Here in the real world,
Where we race to outrun
Everyone through the revolving door,
Hoping that sheer motion
Will sustain us from morning to night.
Utter the seven keys to success,
Explaining why we value progress,
And notice how their hands tremble,
Each finger out of control.
Say it's all within reach
If we just stick to the plan;
Keep our feet steady,
So we're sure to advance.
And speak to them of time—
That little circle on our wrist,
The only watch we can not unwind.

And even when you know
There's no chance of hope,
You still can't let go;
You wash your hands,
Over and over,
But the heart
Never takes well
To a cake of soap
And a basin of water.
Here is a strange new pain,
Which though localized at first,
Spreads slowly from limb to limb,
Until you feel, surely,
This body is not your own;
And how could it be,
When there is nothing
More to touch
But a hard shell
That covers a frozen field.
Somewhere above the tundra,
Foolish voices can be heard
Whispering of seasons to come;
Down the distant hallway,
In a room designed for living,
A man speaks a language
A woman actually understands—
Simple words which occupy
An empty space,
And love is a white bird
With a shattered beak
And a broken wing.

THE WORD

So what if the word went unheard
For a few centuries—
Was it still not the word?
Did God not speak in a tongue
We could fully understand?
Was there not a fundamental plan
Which slowly fell into place,
Before the promised land
Could be called our own;
And when the hideous winds blew,
Did they not whisper our names,
While the steady strain of shame
Spread from continent to continent.

Now we sit, awestruck,
On the brink of a new disaster;
An enemy stands before us,
But he has so many heads
We can not count them all—
So many mouths
We know not which to feed
And which to starve.

Patiently, we wait for a sign,
While all around us
Glows the aftermath of war,
This human struggle to remain
Only what it is we are—
In whose name we exist—
Delaying a lifetime in paradise
For one day on earth.

ABOUT THE AUTHOR

Bart Edelman was born in Paterson, New Jersey, in 1951, and spent his childhood in Teaneck. He received his undergraduate and graduate degrees from Hofstra University. He is currently professor of English at Glendale College, where he edits *Eclipse*, a literary journal. He was awarded grants and fellowships from the United States Department of Education, the University of Southern California and the L.B.J. School of Public Affairs at the University of Texas at Austin, conducting literary research in India, Egypt, Nigeria and Poland. His poetry has appeared in newspapers, journals, textbooks and anthologies. Collections of his work include *Crossing the Hackensack* (1993) and *Under Damaris' Dress* (1996). He lives in Pasadena, California.